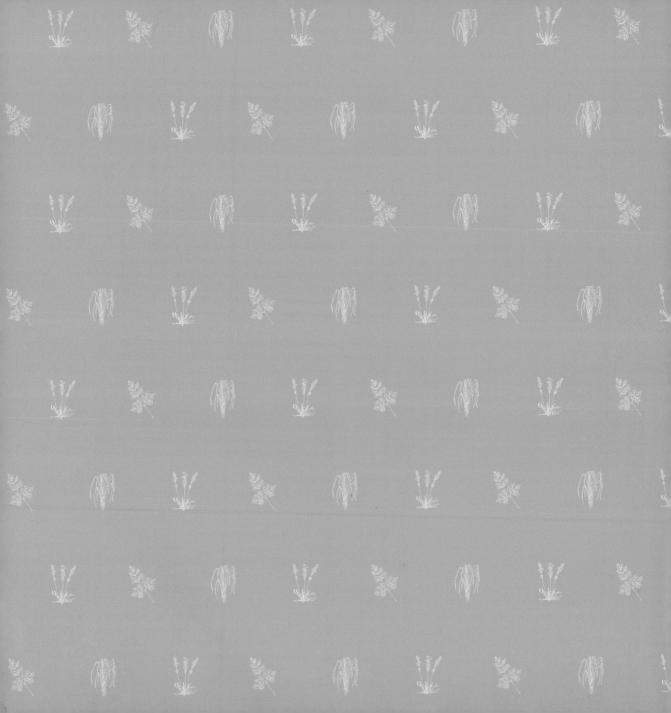

THE HERB BASKET

Lavender

Lovage &
Lemongrass

Levisticum officinale · Cymbopogan citratus · Lavendula officinalis · Lavendula officinalis · citratus · Lavendula officinale · Levisticum officinalis · Lavendula officinale · Cymbopogan citratus · nale ·

THE HERB BASKET

Lavender

Lovage &
Lemongrass

PHOTOGRAPHY BY GLORIA NICOL

Text by Hazel Evans

JG PRESS

THE HERB BASKET
Lavender, Lovage, and Lemongrass

Designed and created by
THE BRIDGEWATER BOOK COMPANY LTD.

Written by Hazel Evans
Photography by Gloria Nicol

Designer: Jane Lanaway
Project editors: Veronica Sperling/Christine McFadden
Page makeup: Chris Lanaway
Step illustrations: Vana Haggerty
Border illustration: Pauline Allen
Cover: Annie Moss
American adaptation: Vicki Power

CLB 4499
© 1996 COLOUR LIBRARY BOOKS LTD
Published in the USA 1996 by JG Press
Distributed by World Publications, Inc.

The JG Press imprint is a trademark of
JG Press, Inc., 455 Somerset Avenue,
North Dighton, MA 02764

Color separation by Tien Wah Press
Printed and bound in Singapore by Tien Wah Press

ISBN 1-57215-110-2

CONTENTS

LAVENDER, LOVAGE, AND LEMONGRASS

THE JOY OF HERBS

Lavender

Lovage

Lemongrass

ERBS ARE the most important plants in our life. They not only give us medicine, but they add color and flavor to the food that we eat, and perfume to the rooms that we live in. And in their own setting they delight the eye: what would an English garden be like in the summer without delicate purple spikes of lavender?

Herbs have always been part of history. One of the largest roles they ever played was in helping the first settlers in America to survive in the new world. In August, 1620 more than a hundred pilgrims set off to settle in what is now the United States. Onboard on that fateful crossing were hundreds of herbs, seeds and plants they needed for survival: not just to provide food and medicine, but to spin for fabrics, and provide fodder for animals.

Most of the early colonists may have had some basic knowledge of plant medicine, but many of them had lived in cities and would have had to learn how to grow things for the first time, and to tend to their own illnesses.

Like her counterpart back in England, the pilgrim housewife used lavender in the new world, not just to perfume her linen, but also to keep moths away from her precious clothes. She also used it as an antiseptic, in oil to massage aching muscles, and as a tea for headaches. It would be rubbed on insect bites and burns. She would also have dried roots of lovage as a cure for rheumatism, and to act as a deodorizer.

Today we are rediscovering the delights of these practical plants. In this little book you'll find dozens of ideas for using three of them: lavender, lovage and lemongrass.

Whether it is to enhance a meal, to perfume your house or to make soothing cream, try these creative ideas – then invent some more of your own.

LAVENDER RINSE

Housewives in the 16th century always rinsed out their linen in lavender. Use a lavender rinse on your finest linen and lingerie for a subtle scent. Boil two handfuls of lavender blooms in a large saucepan of water and leave them to soak overnight. Sieve out the flowers, decant the water into a bowl, and use it as a final rinse for your hand-washed clothes.

11

A lavender field in England.

INTRODUCING LAVENDER

AVENDER is a shrubby plant indigenous to the mountains bordering the Mediterranean. It is believed to have been brought to England by the Romans. Although it has many other uses, lavender is usually associated with perfume. At one time England was famed for the world's finest lavender, but today the country has only one large lavender farm.

Now it is mainly grown and distilled in Provence in southern France, where in summer the landscape is laced with patches of bright purple, and, in the Fall, plumes of purple smoke come from the distillery chimneys nearby.

Several types of lavender are used in the perfume industry. The best is the famous Super Bleue, with flowers of an almost violet hue, which comes from near Mont Ventoux in France. Super Bleue will only grow above 2,500 feet. It provides the basic essence for some of the world's most expensive scents and carries an Appellation d'Origine Contrôlée label, like fine wines.

LAVENDER

Lavender was one of the first herbs to be taken to America by the early settlers. "It is not for this climate" wrote settler John Josselyn in 1672. He was talking about growing it in Maine and northern New England, where it can be cut down in hard winters. Later, the Shakers, a religious sect founded in Manchester, England and who sailed to America in 1773, supported themselves by growing lavender, among other herbs, which they made into medicines and sold, thus starting the world's first pharmaceutical industry. The first Shaker catalogue listed 120 patent medicines for sale; among them was an extract of lavender that was prescribed for flatulence.

At the other end of the scale comes a paler variety called *lavandin,* which is used in more prosaic products – the flowers are used to make soap, kitchen, and bathroom products, while the stalks are used in thermal insulation.

Lavender is an ingredient in the once famous Four Thieves Vinegar, which protected French grave robbers from the plague. The herbalist Parkinson said that lavender is of "especiall good use for all griefes and paines of the head and brain." It was a tradition to wear a quilted cap stuffed with lavender to relieve headaches, and to this day a few drops of lavender oil smoothed on the temples do seem to relieve the pain.

Conserves of lavender used to be set on the table to flavor dishes and "comfort the stomach."

There are more than twenty different kinds of lavender, but the following are the most popular varieties:

COMMON LAVENDER
Lavandula angustifolia

Also known as *L. officinalis* and *L. spica* – called spikenard in ancient times, this is the most popular kind of lavender. It grows to a height of about 32 inches. Hidcote has dark blue flowers and slightly smaller leaves. It is a popular choice for low hedges, growing 18 inches high. Munstead is another short version that also reaches 18 inches. It has purple flowers on spikes that are shorter than other varieties and is also used for hedging, since it spreads rapidly. Twickel Purple, as its names suggests, has deep purple flowers. It grows about 20 inches high.

WHITE LAVENDER
Lavandula angustifolia "Alba"

Common lavender also comes in a white-flowered version that originates in the Alps, and a dwarf white lavender, Nana Alba, which does not grow taller than 12 inches and is good for low edgings around other herbs.

OLD ENGLISH LAVENDER
Lavandula x intermedia

This variety has lighter lavender flowers on longer spikes. The plant grows to approximately 24 inches high.

LAVENDER, LOVAGE, AND LEMONGRASS

COMMON LAVENDER
Lavandula angustifolia

WHITE LAVENDER
Lavandula angustifolia
"Alba"

OLD ENGLISH LAVENDER
Lavandula x *intermedia*

FRENCH LAVENDER
Lavandula stoechas

WOOLY LAVENDER
Lavandula lanata

TOOTHED LAVENDER
Lavandula dentata

FRENCH LAVENDER
Lavandula stoechas

This is a pretty little shrub with narrow leaves and small violet flowers ending in tufts of brightly colored leaflets. This distinctive plant gets its name from the islands of Hyeres in the Mediterranean, which the Romans called Stoechades, where it grows freely. There is a another version called Papillon (*Lavandula stoechas pendunculata*), which has tufted "ears" on top of its blooms. It is not as hardy as other varieties.

WOOLLY LAVENDER
Lavandula lanata

This lavender has distinctive wooly leaves covered in silver-gray down and deep purple flowers on short spikes. It grows to about 20 inches high.

TOOTHED LAVENDER
Lavandula dentata

This has deeply serrated leaves and pale lavender-colored flowers. It comes from the south of Spain and may need some protection in Winter, which is why it is often grown as a houseplant.

15

Lavandula officinalis · Levisticum officinale · Cymbopogon citratus · Lavandula officinalis · Levisticum officinale · Cymbopogon citratus · Lavandula officinalis · Levisticum officinale · Cymbopogon citratus

LAVENDER, LOVAGE, AND LEMONGRASS

INTRODUCING LOVAGE

LOVAGE, ALSO KNOWN as love parsley or sea parsley, is one of the real old English herbs that used to be cultivated in cottage gardens all over England. It tastes like celery and in the past its stalks were often dug up and blanched, too. Lovage is sometimes grown as an ornamental plant in a herbaceous border and can reach up to 7 feet in height in lush conditions.

In some countries lovage is much prized as an aphrodisiac – in Czechoslovakia girls hang a sachet of leaves round their necks when meeting their lovers. The seeds are very pungent and the Greeks and Romans chewed them because they believed it aided digestion. Culpeper said that an infusion of lovage seeds "being dropped into the eyes takes away their redness or dimness."

Native Americans eat lovage raw, but peel the bitter outer stems before they do so. Because it has a very high vitamin C content, sailors used to eat it to avoid getting scurvy on long voyages. Once used in the treatment of rheumatism, the roots were also chewed by country people instead of tobacco.

FAR RIGHT: *Lovage's handsome foliage looks good in a border.*

BELOW: *Lovage makes an attractive foil to flowers.*

LAVENDER, LOVAGE, AND LEMONGRASS

Lovage is widely used in France, Germany, and Italy in soups, casseroles, and stews. The stems can be candied, and they are often used as swizzle sticks for tomato-based drinks, such as Bloody Marys. The seeds, with their strong flavor, are used in Italy and in the U.S. in herb breads and cookies, or powdered and used like a pepper for seasoning. The unusual flavor of lovage – part celery, part yeast – is used commercially as the basis of the famous Maggi soup cubes. In the Middle East, its leaves are chopped into yogurt. In Italy, lovage leaves are put on slices of mozzarella cheese then marinated in olive oil. Lovage also has many uses in the home: the roots can be used to scent bath water and at the same time act as a deodorant, or to aid the circulation and make an invigorating herbal bubble bath.

LOVAGE

*Lovage comes under the astrological
sign of Taurus, the bull, the second sign of
the zodiac. It was used in herbal medicine in
medieval times for stomach disorders,
including colic, and as a gargle
for sore throats.*

INTRODUCING LEMONGRASS

EMONGRASS COMES from Southeast Asia. It is a coarse grass with a bulbous base that looks not unlike large chives, but feels woody and hard, and has a strong smell and tastes of lemon. It needs to be grown in a high temperature, so it can be put outdoors in Summer. It rarely or never bears any flowers and is grown from offsets rather than seeds. Its unique gingery-lemon flavor can be used in both sweet and savory dishes. It can also be infused in hot water as a refreshing drink.

OPPOSITE: *Try growing your own lemongrass – it's handy for oriental dishes.*

BELOW: *Lemongrass ready for harvesting.*

Lemongrass contains citral, an essential oil used in lemon flavorings. It is also used extensively to perfume soaps and colognes. Lemon oil is also used as a massage for stiff joints.

The roots and lower stem are used in oriental dishes in Ceylon, Thailand, Vietnam, and Southeast Asia. Lemongrass goes very well with fish, light meat dishes, and in sweet dishes – try infusing some in milk, then adding it to a rice pudding.

To release their volatile oils, the roots and lower stem need to be crushed or chopped before adding to a dish.

You can also find lemongrass in powder form. An infusion of crushed stems makes a

LEMONGRASS BOUQUET GARNI

The outer leaves are used like a bouquet garni — put a bunch into a slow-cooking dish, then remove it just before serving.

lemon-flavored tisane that is very refreshing served poured over cracked ice cubes. It is also used in India, infused in milk, as a calming medicine for feverish patients.

Lemongrass is well worth growing for yourself to give a new and exciting taste to your cooking. It has another valuable property: in Thailand it is believed that having lemongrass in the house brings good luck to all members of the family.

TIP
If you have difficulty finding supplies of lemongrass, substitute slivers of lemon peel in marinades, curries, and casseroles. In salads use the chopped leaves of lemon balm, a hardy herb that is easy to grow in the garden.

LAVENDER, LOVAGE, AND LEMONGRASS

PLANT CARE

N O HERB GARDEN should be complete without lavender and lovage. Apart from their many uses, they both have beautiful foliage – lavender's silvery needle-like leaves contrast beautifully with the glossy dark green stems of lovage. Coming from a tropical climate, lemongrass needs to be grown indoors, but its bamboo-like shoots look good on a kitchen windowsill.

To grow lavender from cuttings, put several in one pot. To speed up rooting, put wire hoops over them and cover with a "tent" made out of a clear plastic sandwich bag.

LAVENDER
Lavandula

A hardy evergreen shrub (but *stoechas* and *lanata* are tender varieties). It can grow up to 4 feet but there are many compact varieties available. Lavender prefers sunshine and likes a light, well-drained soil that is not too rich. Put lavender plants 2 feet apart. Sow lavender seeds on the surface of the soil in a seed tray in the Fall and give them some bottom heat if you can. Transfer the seedlings into pots containing well-drained compost; keep them in a cold greenhouse or cold frame until the Spring. Let the roots get well established before you put them in the ground.

Lavender roots very easily. Take ripe cuttings in the Fall, setting several into a pot. Leave young plants indoors to overwinter.

Lavender should be cut back hard in the spring and trimmed after flowering.

LOVAGE
Levisticum officinale

This hardy perennial can grow up to 6 feet in height. It can take partial shade and thrives in a moist fertile soil, but its roots should be protected in severe Winters. Set your lovage plants 2 feet apart. Keep them well watered for fresh supplies of foliage.

Sow seeds outdoors in the Fall and thin out in the Spring. Take off the flowers as they appear to allow the roots to swell if you are using them for cookery. But allow some plants to flower in order to save the seeds.

Divide the clumps in the autumn and remove the large outside leaves.

LEMONGRASS
Cymbopogon citratus

This perennial tropical grass grows like bamboo and achieves a height of up to 6 feet in tropical conditions, but no more than 3 feet in a container.

Lemongrass is normally grown from offsets planted in the Spring.

The easiest way to raise your own is to buy some fresh lemongrass from an ethnic grocer or supermarket and put it in water, where it should sprout roots.

Lemongrass needs a temperature above 56 degrees at all times. It prefers a rich water-retentive soil (avoid lightweight composts) and needs constant moisture – mist it frequently and divide large clumps in the Fall.

SPLITTING A LOVAGE PLANT

When it has formed a large clump, lovage can be divided. Simply plunge two small hand forks, back to back, into the center of the plant and pull them apart. If the clump is very large and the roots tough, you could chop it in half with a spade.

HOW TO PROPAGATE LEMONGRASS

You can raise your own with lemongrass bought from a shop, but make sure it is green and fresh-looking. Suspend a bundle in water until it sprouts whiskery roots, then transfer to pots (see page 31).

HARVESTING

ATHER THE FLOWERS of lavender early in the day, but after any dew has dried off them. Cut the stems at the base, even if you are planning to use only the tips; it will make the plant look tidier, and the stems can be stored and used on open fires and in stoves.

ABOVE: *The delicate flowers of French lavender are easier to harvest if it is grown in a pot, like this specimen.*

A LAVENDER RACK

Pick the flowers just before they are fully open, and tie the lavender spikes into bunches, ready for drying. It is easy to make a crisscross rack for lavender using twigs lashed together with raffia and suspended on hooks. If you are making lavender sheaves (see page 46), stand them upright to dry. Keep lavender flowers away from direct sunlight or they will fade.

22

LAVENDER, LOVAGE, AND LEMONGRASS

LEFT: *Always harvest herbs like lemongrass, lovage, and lavender freshly if you are planning to preserve them. Deal with them immediately.*

Cut lovage leaves fresh from the plant as you need them. Snip from the center, as the outside leaves become coarse and tasteless in time. If you are planning to use the base of lovage stems and roots for cooking, earth up around the base of the plant to blanch it, which will take out the bitterness. Use a sharp knife to detach pieces for cooking. Replace the soil carefully afterwards.

Cut lemongrass as you want to use it for cooking. The fresh young green tips can be snipped off with scissors to chop and use in salads and other uncooked dishes. If it is grown in a decorative pot, bring the lemongrass straight to the table and let guests help themselves from the plant.

The lower part of the stem should be carefully cut or detached at soil level and used for longer cooked dishes – tie several together and put them to cook with meat in casseroles and curries, then remove before serving.

LAVENDER, LOVAGE, AND LEMONGRASS

PRESERVING

LAVENDER DRIES VERY easily. Tie the spikes into bunches and hang them upside down in a warm, dark place. The process normally takes about fourteen days. To speed things up you can dry the stems individually on cake racks, or in small bunches of five or six spikes at a time poked through holes in a chicken wire frame.

Lavender flowers will keep their fragrance for up to five years under wraps. The best way to store them is in paper bags. The actual flowers have no fragrance – it is the tiny green bracts at their base that give off the aroma.

To dry lavender leaves for potpourris, sachets and bath bags, hang up the stems for five days to harden them a little, then strip off the leaves into paper bags and store in an open, well-ventilated place.

Tie stems of lovage together and hang them up to dry or lay them out on wire racks. The leaves, which have the most flavor, will dry before the stems. Crumble them on to a sheet of paper, then decant them into glass jars. Lovage leaves can also be frozen successfully in small plastic bags.

RIGHT: *Lavender, lovage, and lemongrass all preserve well.*

LEMONGRASS

This herb comes under the earth sign of Capricorn, and has the protection of the Dragon in ancient oriental astrology.

The young green tips of lemongrass can be put into plastic sandwich bags and then frozen. Flatten the bag with the palm of your hand to expel as much air as possible. Alternatively they can be frozen in little parcels made up from aluminum foil.

The whole plant can be dried, then crumbled. This is best done in a low oven with the door open, or in a linen closet, which is a longer process. Split the stems lengthwise and spread them on wax paper on a plate or a board. They will take at least two weeks to dry. They can eventually be crumbled and put into jars. Store them in a cool dark place and use within six months.

LEFT: *The easiest way to preserve lemongrass is to freeze it in plastic bags. Dried lemongrass can be used in place of fresh leaves in cooking, but the flavor will be much more pungent, so quantities should be reduced.*

25

The bold colors of lavender and rose beneath a decorative seat.

PLANNING A HERB GARDEN

DIAMOND 2
Thyme

DIAMOND 1
Sage

DIAMOND 3
Rosemary

DIAMOND 4
Lavender

T HE HERB garden (above) is based on a simple set of diamonds and can be as large or as small as you please. It would look good set in the middle of an existing lawn, for instance, and is a good shape to show off larger specimens such as lovage and lavender. Each diamond features a different family of herbs, but they could equally well be divided into dye plants, medicinal plants, those for teas and tisanes, and for cookery. Adapt the garden to suit yourself, adding and subtracting the diamonds as you wish, adding triangles as extra beds on the edge. The diamonds can be any size

you like, but the minimum measurement should be 24 inches square, with an allowance of 16 inches between them as a footpath. Lovage is grown as a feature plant in a handsome urn in the center.

Lavender lends itself particularly well to planting on a grand scale. If the plants are set out in a geometric pattern and kept in clipped ball shapes, they can make very decorative patterns. Planted in lines they also make a useful break between stronger growing herbs like mint and lemon balm, stopping them from overwhelming the others.

PLANTING A LAVENDER HEDGE

A HERBAL HEDGE not only makes an aromatic edge to a herb garden, but looks good around a flower border, too. The quickest and easiest way of creating a lavender hedge is to make one from container-grown cuttings which you have taken yourself or bought from a nursery.

TIP
Water your hedging plants well in the first few weeks. Remember, when they are fully grown they will need watering in periods of drought, as the thick bushy growth will stop moisture reaching the roots.

1. Use a length of twine and two pegs to mark a straight line, or a length of hose to make a curve, and make a row of holes where your plants are to go. Sprinkle a little organic fertilizer in and around the site.

2. Working as quickly as possible so that the roots are not exposed to the elements, set your plants into the ground. Full-size lavenders should be set 24 inches apart, smaller varieties like Munstead about 12 inches apart.

3. Clip the tops regularly to encourage side growth. Once the hedge is established, cut it back severely each Spring, and, as it grows, trim it so that the sides slope a little and the base is broader than the top.

Lavender looks good in a border.

Lemongrass makes amusing "hair" for a pot on which a face has been painted.

INDOOR HERBS

ALL KINDS OF lavender, but especially the half-hardy varieties, will thrive indoors. Their stalks are pliable enough to be espaliered on little wire frames or trained onto a hoop. Choose young plants, as they are easier to handle.

Lemongrass looks its best in a decorative container rather than in an ordinary pot, which tends to emphasize its stiff appearance. Try it instead in white jars or bowls. Lemongrass looks amusing used as the "hair" in a pot in the shape of a head. It looks good, too, set off by oriental containers of any kind: Chinese bowls, for instance, ginger jars, or dragon pots. Lemongrass also goes well with bright, polished brass. Keep your plants in their original pots and sink them inside containers filled with vermiculite or some other "clean" growing medium. You can then take them out when you need to water them, or harvest some of the stalks.

1. Use broken crocks for drainage if you are planting directly into a container, and a growing medium like perlite or vermiculite to conceal interior pots.

2. If it is bare-rooted, plant the lemongrass in the container rather than in a pot. Take care not to damage the whiskery roots, which break easily.

ABOVE: *Plant lavender in pots and bring indoors in Winter. Their fragrance will perfume a room.*

Lavandula officinalis · Levisticum officinale ·

LAVENDER, LOVAGE, AND LEMONGRASS

ORIENTAL SALAD

BOTH LOVAGE and lemongrass make flavorful additions to salads. Use the torn leaves of lovage instead of celery, which it resembles in taste. Don't be heavy-handed, however – get to know it first, for its leaves are very pungent. For a milder flavor, rub the leaves around a wooden salad bowl as you would a cut clove of garlic. Chop the tips of young shoots of lemongrass over exotic oriental salads like this one. Snip lemongrass over rice-based dishes for a subtle lemon flavor.

INGREDIENTS

Serves 4

4 ounces snow peas

4 ounces baby corncobs

1 iceberg lettuce

½ red pepper

4 scallions

2 young carrots

4 ounces button mushrooms

2 tbs chopped lemongrass tips

4 lovage leaves

vinaigrette dressing

1 tsp honey

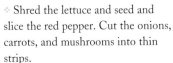

❖ Dip the snow peas and corncobs in boiling water for 1 minute to blanch them, then drain and cool.

❖ Shred the lettuce and seed and slice the red pepper. Cut the onions, carrots, and mushrooms into thin strips.

❖ Combine in a salad bowl with the peas, corn, lemongrass, and torn lovage leaves.

❖ Top the salad with a vinaigrette dressing with a teaspoonful of honey beaten in.

TIP

If you like a spicy vinaigrette, add a teaspoonful of wholegrain mustard as well as honey to the mix.

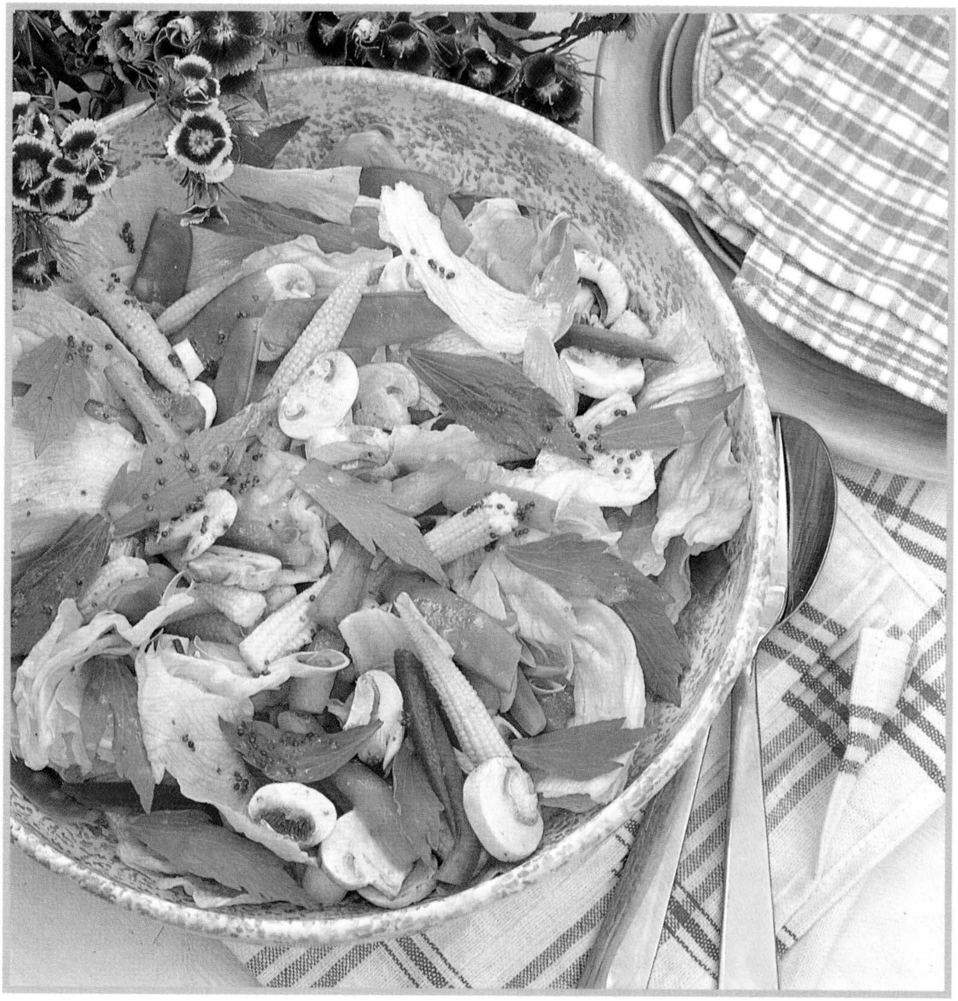

Lavandula officinalis · Levisticum officinale · Cymbopogon citratus · Lavandula officinalis · Levisticum officinale · Cymbopogon citratus · Lavandula · Levisticum officinale · Cymbopogon citratus

LAVENDER, LOVAGE, AND LEMONGRASS

COOKING WITH LOVAGE

THE STRONG AND distinctly celery-like flavor of lovage goes well in soups and casseroles, and can be used instead of vine leaves to encase meat. Wrap its leaves around fish, too, before cooking it on a grill or barbecue. Add chopped lovage leaves to cheese and hollandaise sauces or mix them with melted butter to baste chicken dishes.

CREAM OF LOVAGE SOUP

INGREDIENTS

Serves 4

1 large onion
8 oounces potatoes
2 tbs butter
4 tbs finely chopped lovage leaves
3⅓ cups chicken stock
⅔ cup heavy cream

❖ Finely chop the onion, then peel, slice and chop the potatoes. Melt the butter in a heavy saucepan and fry the onion until soft, but not brown. Stir in the lovage leaves and cook for a few seconds until they go limp. Add the chopped potatoes and the chicken stock, season, and cook for 25 minutes. Blend in a food processor, then return to the saucepan. Stir in the cream, season and reheat to simmering point, but do not boil. Serve immediately.

❖ If you want a less calorie-rich soup, omit the cream and stir in some lowfat yogurt or crème fraîche just before serving. For a different summery flavor, add 2 tablespoonfuls of fresh orange juice just before serving.

TIP

This soup is excellent served chilled
in Summer. Keep it in the fridge for at
least an hour before serving.

STUFFED LOVAGE LEAVES

THIS RECIPE makes a delicious change from dolmades. Lovage leaves, unlike vine leaves, impart their own delicate flavor to the meat. For a spicier taste, you could add some crushed garlic and a good pinch of chili powder to the tomato sauce .

INGREDIENTS

Serves 4

bunch of large lovage leaves
1 onion
1 tbs olive oil
pinch of ground cumin powder
6 ounces minced cooked lean lamb
¹/₄ cup seasoned cooked rice
1-pound can chopped tomatoes

❧ Lay the lovage leaves in a deep plate or casserole, pour over boiling water and leave them to soften. Drain and blot dry. Chop the onion finely and cook in the oil in a heavy pan. Sprinkle over the cumin, stir in the lamb and rice and cook until well blended. Season well and set aside.

❧ Cut some aluminum foil into eight 5-inch squares. Arrange the lovage leaves over the squares so that the foil is completely covered. Put a tablespoonful of the lamb mixture in the center of each square and roll up securely, tucking in the ends.

❧ Pack the rolls together in an ovenproof dish and bake in a preheated oven at 400 degrees for 30 minutes. Meanwhile, drain then heat the canned tomatoes in a saucepan, crushing them to a thick sauce with a potato masher. Season with salt and pepper.

❧ Carefully remove the aluminum foil from the lovage leaf rolls, and serve them surrounded by the tomato sauce.

Lavandula officinalis · Levisticum officinale · Cymbopogon citratus · Lavandula officinalis · Levisticum officinale · Cymbopogon citratus · Lavandula officinalis · Levisticum officinale · Cymbopogon citratus · Lavandula officinalis

LAVENDER, LOVAGE, AND LEMONGRASS

THAI STIR-FRY WITH LOVAGE AND LEMONGRASS

T HIS SPICY DISH should be served with rice. You can infuse lemongrass shoots in the boiling water in which the rice is cooked to give it an extra lemon taste.

INGREDIENTS

Serves 4

4 ounces fillet or rump steak
1-inch piece fresh ginger root
juice of 1 lemon
3 tbs sherry
$\frac{1}{2}$ tsp chili powder
6 tbs crunchy peanut butter
2 cloves garlic, crushed
1 onion
1 red pepper
2 tbs oil
4 ounces green beans
2 tbs chopped lemongrass tips
1 tbs chopped lovage leaves
1 cup frozen peas
$\frac{3}{4}$ cup Greek-style yogurt

TIP

Cook rice in meat stock for extra flavour, then to remove any stickiness, pour boiling water over it, and drain thoroughly.

✧ Cut the steak into thin strips with a sharp knife. Place in a bowl. Peel and chop the ginger and mix with the lemon juice, sherry, chili powder, peanut butter, and garlic. Season with salt and pepper, pour over the meat strips, stir well, and leave to marinate for 30 minutes.

✧ Cut the onion into quarters and then into slices. Seed the red pepper and cut it into strips.

✧ Heat the oil in a deep frying pan or wok, and stir-fry the onion, pepper, green beans, lemongrass, and lovage for 3 minutes. Add the steak and the marinade and continue frying until the meat is well cooked – about 5 minutes. Add the frozen peas and cook for a further 5 minutes until they are thoroughly heated through.

✧ Serve on a bed of rice, putting a spoonful of yogurt on each serving of stir-fry.

37

LOVAGE AND CARROT QUICHE

L OVAGE GOES well with eggs, cheese, and cream. It can be added to the classic Quiche Lorraine, but here is a different version. You can also add lovage to boiled or steamed carrots to bring out their flavor.

SHORTCRUST PASTRY

The classic recipe for shortcrust pastry is half fat to flour. A mix of margarine and lard gives the best texture. The type of flour you use will dictate how your shortcrust pastry behaves. Always add a pinch of salt. For a crunchier result, use half wholewheat flour, half white flour. In this case, use self-raising white flour as the wholewheat tends to make the pastry rather heavy.

TIP

When baking blind, brush the base of the quiche with beaten egg to seal it and keep the pastry crisp when the filling is added.

INGREDIENTS

Serves 4

8 ounces shortcrust pastry
1 pound young carrots
$1/4$ cup butter
1 tbs chopped lovage leaves
$1/2$ cup grated Cheddar cheese
2 eggs, beaten
$1 1/4$ cups cream

❖ Roll out and bake the pastry blind in a flan tin.
❖ Clean the carrots and slice into thin discs. Fry them in the butter for 2 or 3 minutes, add 1 tablespoon water and simmer until they are just cooked but still firm – about 10 minutes.
❖ Remove from the heat, stir in the chopped lovage, grated cheese, beaten eggs, and cream. Pour the mixture into the pastry case. Bake for 30 minutes in a preheated oven at 400 degrees. Serve piping hot, sprinkled with chopped fresh lovage.

LAVENDER, LOVAGE, AND LEMONGRASS

39

LAVENDER ICE CREAM

AVENDER CAN be used to make some stunning desserts. It is especially good with ice cream. Try it, too, in milk-based puddings. If necessary, you can substitute dried lavender flowers for fresh ones, but if you do, halve the quantity – don't forget, the flavor of lavender is as powerful as rosemary.

TIP

This ice cream and the cookies opposite can also be made with rosemary flowers for a completely different, but delightful, flavor.

INGREDIENTS

Serves 4
6 spikes lavender flowers
1 egg
²⁄₃ cup milk
3 tbs sugar
¹⁄₂ tsp vanilla essence
²⁄₃ cup heavy cream

❖ Strip the lavender flowers off their stems. Beat the egg. Heat the milk and sugar together with the lavender flowers, and allow to infuse for 20 minutes. Pour the infused milk onto the egg, stirring as you go. Return the mixture to the pan and reheat, stirring all the time until it thickens.
❖ Strain into a bowl and add the vanilla essence. Allow the custard to cool, then half-whip the cream and fold it into the mixture. Spoon into an ice cream maker or freeze in a container in your freezer, giving it a stir after about 30 minutes.
❖ Serve the ice cream garnished with lavender sprigs.

LAVENDER COOKIES

UT THESE cookies into pretty shapes and
serve them with ice cream or fresh fruit
salads. Alternatively, hand a plate of cookies
around to accompany fruits poached in a
lemon-flavored lavender syrup.

INGREDIENTS
Makes about 24
¹/₂ cup butter or margarine
²/₃ cup sugar
1 egg yolk
2 tbs lavender leaves
1²/₃ cups flour
grated rind of 1 lemon
2 tsp lavender flowers

❀ Cream the fat and sugar until pale and fluffy.
Add the egg yolk and beat well. Finely chop the
lavender leaves and mix them with the flour and
grated lemon rind. Stir the flour mix into the
creamed fat to make a firm dough. Roll out to
about ¹/₄ inch thickness, sprinkling it with tiny
lavender flowers as you go. Cut into fancy shapes
with cookie cutters. Transfer the cookies to
greased baking sheets and bake in a preheated
oven at 350 degrees for about 15 minutes or
until pale golden brown. Place on a wire rack
to cool, then keep in an airtight tin.

Lavandula officinalis · Levisticum officinale · Cymbopogon citratus · Lavandula officinalis · Levisticum officinale · Cymbopogon citratus · Lavandula officinalis · Levisticum officinale · Cymbopogon citratus ·

LAVENDER, LOVAGE, AND LEMONGRASS

SYRUPS AND CORDIALS

LAVENDER, lovage, and lemongrass make syrups and cordials that should have a place in every store cupboard. Try them in tisane form, too. The stems of lovage can also be candied in a similar way to angelica.

LAVENDER SYRUP

TRY SPOONING this delicious lavender syrup over ice creams, sorbets, pancakes or fresh fruit. Use it, too, as a refreshing drink: pour some over cracked ice in a tall glass, then add soda water.

INGREDIENTS
Makes 2$\frac{1}{2}$ cups
handful of lavender flowers
1$\frac{3}{4}$ cups sugar

❧ Put the flowers in a saucepan with 2$\frac{1}{2}$ cups water. Bring to the boil, then remove from the heat. Cover and leave overnight.
❧ Strain the liquid over the sugar in a heavy pan and bring slowly to the boil, stirring as you go. When the sugar has completely dissolved, turn up the heat and cook rapidly until it thickens but does not color. Allow to cool slightly, then put into sterilized bottles.

LOVAGE CORDIAL

THE DRINK known as lovage that was sold in English public houses in Victorian times did not contain lovage at all, but was made with tansy. This cordial makes a splendid *digestif*, as the French call it, a drink to settle the stomach and help the meal go down.

INGREDIENTS
Makes 1 bottle
2 tbs lovage seeds
1 bottle inexpensive brandy

❧ Pour the seeds into the bottle of brandy and allow to them to steep for a week, then drain and rebottle.

TO MAKE
A TISANE

Lemongrass can be used to make a cooling drink for hot summer days: simply steep a bunch o f shoots in 2½ cups boiling water, allow it to cool, then strain and pour over ice cubes.

43

LAVENDER, LOVAGE, AND LEMONGRASS

HERB OILS

B OTH LOVAGE and lemongrass can be used to make
delicious herb oils. Use them in cooking – fry meat
or spices in lemongrass oil, use lovage oil to sweat the onions
for a soup and to make unusual salad dressings.
When making these herb oils it is best to use a bland
base, such as peanut or sunflower, rather than olive
oil, as its taste would be too intrusive.

LOVAGE OIL

INGREDIENTS

Makes 2 cups
bunch of fresh young lovage leaves
2 cups sunflower oil

⁕ Crush the leaves with a mortar and pestle,
add a little of the oil and crush them again.
Continue until half the oil is used up, then
transfer the mix to a bottle. Add the remaining
oil and shake. If you do not have a mortar and
pestle you can use a food processor, but only
blend very briefly (for the count of five) or the
oil will become hazy.
⁕ Leave the bottle on a sunny windowsill or in a
warm place, giving it a shake from time to time.
After two weeks, strain the oil through muslin,
pour it into a fresh bottle and add a sprig of
fresh lovage for decoration.

LEMONGRASS OIL

INGREDIENTS

Makes 2 cups
handful of lemongrass stalks
2 cups sunflower oil

⁕ Lay the lemongrass stalks on a wooden
board and crush them lightly with a hammer
wrapped in a piece of muslin. It is essential to
bruise the stalks this way in order to extract
the essential oils.
⁕ Place them in a wide-necked bottle, warm the
oil to blood heat and carefully pour over the
lemongrass.
⁕ Leave the mix for at least one month in a warm
place, shaking the bottle from time to time.
⁕ Pour off the oil through muslin into a fresh
bottle, add a slice of lemon for decoration and
seal tightly.

Lavandula officinalis · Levisticum officinale · Cymbopogon citratus · Levisticum officinale · Cymbopogon citratus · Lavandula officinalis · Levisticum officinale · Cymbopogon citratus · Lavandula officinalis

LAVENDER, LOVAGE, AND LEMONGRASS

A DRIED LAVENDER SHEAF

HEAVES OF DRIED lavender look very chic, but cost a great deal. Here's how to make one for yourself at a fraction of the price. Harvest the lavender when it is at its best – when the flowers are just about to come out.

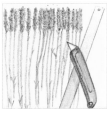

1. Lay the lavender spikes on a board, matching up their tips so that they are exactly in line with each other.

TIP
If you leave the harvested lavender spikes to dry and harden for a day or two before using, they are easier to handle.

2. Measure the length of the stalks by placing your chosen container a suitable distance from the tips. Then trim the base of the stalks. Secure with a rubber band. Stand somewhere warm and well ventilated to dry, out of direct light.

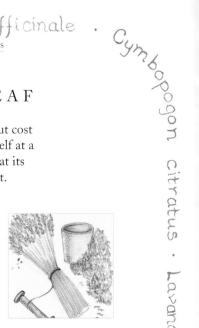

3. When the lavender is completely dry, wrap the middle of the spikes with a piece of florist's wire, taking care it does not cut into the stems. Push the stems into a pot containing moss.

AROMATIC MATS

IT'S PLEASANT to smell the aroma of lemon or lavender as you set a hot pan or teapot down on the kitchen table. And it's easy to achieve with these pretty quilted place mats stuffed with fragrant dried lavender or lemongrass. They make welcome gifts. Collect attractive fabric remnants to make them with, choosing a plain or contrasting patterned fabric for the backing.

MATERIALS

Makes 1

square of decorative fabric 10 × 10 inches
square of backing fabric (felt or plain cotton)
the same size
square of thin wadding the same size
good handful of dried lavender or lemongrass
length of bias binding 30 inches long
some dressmaking chalk

1. Cut out the scalloped shape in the top fabric, backing fabric and wadding. Seam them together, leaving a space for the stuffing. Draw on guidelines for quilting in chalk on one side.

2. Stuff with dried lavender or dried lemongrass. Seam up the gap by hand.

3. Keeping it flat so the stuffing does not shift, quilt the mat carefully by hand or machine along the chalk lines.

4. Pin then stitch the bias binding to the edges of the front of the mat.

49

Lavandula officinalis · Levisticum officinale · Cymbopogon citratus · Lavandula officinalis · Levisticum officinale · Cymbopogon citratus

LAVENDER, LOVAGE, AND LEMONGRASS

AROMATIC OILS

T IP
Aromatic oils
have practical uses,
too: mix oil of lavender
with oils of peppermint
and basil to give an
aroma that helps
clear the sinuses.

USE AROMATIC oils and lavender-scented joss sticks to perfume the air. Essential oils can be used in atomizers and oil burners, too, placed around the room. Try them in the water in humidifiers hung on radiators; the warmth will release their scent. Put a few drops of oil into a centerpiece for a dinner party – a bowl of water with floating flower candles in it.

⬧ A mix of lavender with hyssop pine and rosemary is said to be good for anyone with breathing problems.
⬧ Mix a few drops of herbal oil with a little water and set it in a bowl over a nightlight to scent the air.
⬧ Put some drops of oil of lavender in a saucer of warm water on a windowsill to freshen the room.

Lavandula officinalis · Levisticum officinale · Cymbopogon citratus · Lavandula officinalis · Levisticum officinale · Cymbopogon citratus · Lavandula officinalis · Levisticum officinale · Cymbopogon citratus · Lavandula officinalis

LAVENDER, LOVAGE, AND LEMONGRASS

FIRE BUNDLES

LAVENDER

Shakespeare called it "hot lavender" because of its warming scent. Culpeper says its oil "is of a fierce and piercing quality, a very few drops being sufficient for inward or outward maladies."

NEVER THROW away the stalks of lavender when you prune or trim your plants. Stack them in bundles and throw them on an open fire for heady, perfumed smoke. They work well in wood-burning stoves, too.
Store your sticks in the dark, away from sunlight, which might otherwise leach out the perfumed oils in the stem.

LAVENDER, LOVAGE, AND LEMONGRASS

Lavandula officinalis · Levisticum officinale · Cymbopogon citratus · Lavandula officinalis · Levisticum officinale · Cymbopogon citratus · Lavandula officinalis · Levisticum

LAVENDER, LOVAGE, AND LEMONGRASS

HERBAL BUBBLE BATH

B OTH LAVENDER and lemongrass can be used to make your own bubble bath and toilet waters – lavender to stimulate the skin, lemongrass to soothe it. Substitute or add other herbs, too, to make your own personal versions. Start collecting decorative antique glass bottles to keep your bath and toilet waters in.

INGREDIENTS

Makes 2¹⁄₂ cups

*1¹⁄₄ cups top quality unperfumed
dishwashing liquid*

1¹⁄₄ cups distilled water

4 drops essential oil of lavender or lemongrass

2 drops blue or yellow food coloring (optional)

1. Pour the ingredients into a 2¹⁄₂ cup container and shake thoroughly, then put into a decorative bath bottle.

PERFUME

*The word perfume comes from the
Latin per fume – "through fire." The first
scents were the aromatic woods
burned in their temples.*

LAVENDER WATER

U SE LAVENDER water to give a delicious scent to a bath, or as a personal perfume. Keep a bottle in the fridge in summer so that you can dip a handkerchief into it to cool your brow.

INGREDIENTS

Makes 2²⁄₃ cups

2¹⁄₂ cups distilled water

¹⁄₄ cup vodka

8 drops essential oil of lavender

1. Shake the ingredients together thoroughly in a container, then decant into decorative bottles.

LAVENDER SCENTED INK

IN ANCIENT times, inks were made from natural ingredients such as galls from oak trees. An infusion of these was used to color water with which to write. The inks were then fixed with the use of gum arabic. Make your own scented inks the easy way by simply adding a little essential oil of lavender or a strong infusion you have made yourself. Choose inks that are an appropriate blue tone.

1. Add two drops of essential oil of lavender to a bottle of ink and leave it for several days before using.

2. Alternatively, you can make a very strong infusion of the herb by just covering a cupful of lavender with boiling water. Leave to cool overnight, drain off the liquid and add a teaspoonful to a bottle of ink.

LAVENDER SCENTED PAPERS

YOU CAN MAKE papers completely from a pulp of freshly cut herbs, but it is a complicated, messy task that takes a long time. You also have to use caustic soda, which gives off fumes. Instead, it is far easier to buy attractive handmade paper and scent it yourself. If you use the second method, below, you could also color your notepaper by putting a drop of ink in the water.

1. Store your most precious writing paper interleaved with lavender in boxes.

2. For a stronger effect and a more rustic look, add two or three drops of essential oil of lavender to a bowl of water. Dip sheets of plain writing paper in the scented water and hang them up to dry.

LAVENDER, LOVAGE, AND LEMONGRASS

LAVENDER, LOVAGE, AND LEMONGRASS

LAVENDER SLEEP TOYS

C HILDREN LOVE lavender-scented sleep toys to tuck under their pillows. They are simple to do and make good stocking fillers at Christmas time.

MATERIALS

*scraps of brightly colored patterned fabric
simple paper animal shapes (the easiest are teddy bears
and pussy cats; older children could draw their own)
dried lavender flowers*

1. Lay the animal shapes on the fabric, and draw around them with dressmaking chalk or pen, leaving ¼ inch all around for a seam allowance.

2. Right sides together, sew round the shape, leaving a space at the bottom to take the stuffing.

3. Turn the shape right side out, stuff firmly with lavender, using a knitting needle to poke the herb into tricky corners like ears.

4. Sew up the gap. Add a woolen tail if appropriate.

57

Lavandula officinalis · Levisticum officinale · Cymbopogon citratus · Lavandula officinalis · Levisticum officinale · Lavandula officinalis · Cymbopogon citratus · Cymbopogon citratus · Levisticum officinale ·

LAVENDER, LOVAGE, AND LEMONGRASS

SHOE SHAPERS

O RDINARY SHOE trees can be padded with wadding scented with lavender oil, or encased in a bag filled with dried lavender flowers. Alternatively, using the toe of the shoe tree as a guide, make a paper pattern for push-in shoe shapers – little bags of lavender to poke inside your shoes.

MATERIALS

Makes 1 pair
paper pattern
4 pieces decorative fabric
2 handfuls dried lavender flowers
ribbon

3. Insert a ribbon loop in the center and stitch in place.

1. Using your pattern, cut out 4 shapes in fabric, pin their right sides together, then tack.

2. Sew the curved sides, leaving the end open. Trim, turn right side out, and stuff with lavender. Hand sew the end, leaving a gap in the center.

A SHOE BAG

A LAVENDER-SCENTED shoe bag is both pretty and practical, for it has a deodorizing effect. Stitch decorative fabric into a bag shape, thread a piece of cord through the top, and knot the ends. Make up a 3 inch-deep muslin bag to the same width. Fill with lavender and sew on all sides. Stitch into the base of the shoe bag.

59

Lavandula officinalis · Levisticum officinale · Cymbopogon citratus · Lavandula officinalis · Levisticum officinale · Cymbopogon citratus · Lavandula officinalis · Levisticum officinale

LAVENDER, LOVAGE, AND LEMONGRASS

INDEX

ACKNOWLEDGMENTS

The publishers would like to thank
the following companies for their help:

BASKETS AND GLASSWARE
Global Village,
Sparrow Works, Bower Hinton, Martock, Somerset.
Telephone: +44 (1935) 823390

DRIED HERBS AND FLOWERS
The Hop Shop,
Castle Farm, Shoreham, Sevenoaks, Kent TN14 7UB.
Telephone: +44 (1959) 523219

HERB PLANTS BY MAIL ORDER
Jekka's Herb Farm,
Rose Cottage, Shellards Lane, Alveston, Bristol BS12 2SY.
Telephone: +44 (1454) 418878

HERB SEEDS
Suffolk Seeds,
Monks Farm, Pantlings Lane, Coggeshall Road,
Kelvedon, Essex CO5 9PG.
Telephone: +44 (1376) 572456

PICTURE CREDITS
Andrew Lawson Photography; p.15ML
S & O Matthews Photography: p.26
Photos Horticultural: pp.12, 15TR, BL and BR, 18
Harry Smith Collection: p.15TL

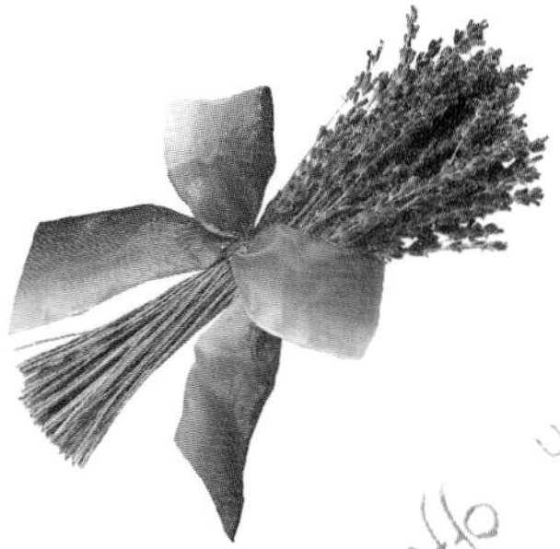